IS IT JUNE YET ?

THE MUSINGS OF THE BEMUSED:
A VETERAN TEACHER'S PERSPECTIVE

By Pam Felcher

I have taught for over 30 years in public and private school, religious school, college and university. After two ten-year stints teaching in the District, I decided to document the ups, downs, problems, solutions, along with the humorous and not so humorous situations I experienced during my last year teaching in public school. The last entries are reflections written during my first year at the school I moved to after deciding once and for all that enough was enough. . . at least for now. I like to think I teach the free communication of ideas, and I believe in practicing what I preach, so here goes. . . .

Table of Contents:

The First First Day. 5

ANXIETY:
Scores Walk in (8/3). 10
CLAD or unCLAD? That is
the Question! (8/11). 13
Quality of Life (8/18). 18
A Retiree's Vision (8/24). 25
Separation Anxiety (8/31). 30

REALITY:
Day 1 (9/9). 32
What is Access Anyway (8/8). 34
Selecting AP Teachers. Who decides?
And How? (8/10). 38
One Week Down—Thirty-Nine
to Go (9/11). 41
Summon(s)ed by a Higher Power? (9/28). . . 43
It Started with a Giggle . . . (10/12). 45
Evaluating the Evaluators (10/18). 48
(IN)Adequate (10/20). 51
There's No Biz Like Ed Biz (10/25). 54
La Dolce Vita (11/3). 58
Finger-Lickin' Obnoxious (11/11). 62
"The Thousand Natural Shocks that
Flesh is Heir to" (12/17). 67
The Sublime to the Delicious (2/6). 71

Test-Score Tyranny (3/6). 74
Land of Nod (4/11). 77
NY Loves Me, Me, Me, Me . . . (5/6). 82
Grating Grading (5/7). 85
Rigor. . . Mortis (5/21). 89
"And You All Know, Security is Mortals'
Chiefest Enemy" (6/12). 93
Recycling, 101 (6/19). 95

REFLECTIONS:
Rewards Points (1/10). 100
I Could Have Danced All Night (1/13). . . . 104
What's Love Got to Do With It? (3/9). . . . 108
Plays Well With Others (6/26). 113
Yup, It's June! (6/28). 118

EPILOGUE. 121

DEDICATION. 122

THE FIRST FIRST DAY

When I first entered the hallowed halls of public school back in 1986, I had a sense of what was in store. In the 50s my mother had been a teacher at a pretty rough New York City high school for about six months until she married. She warned me about the rigidly inadequate system, filled with complacent teachers and angry students. Being the detritus of the feminist movement, I knew I would not be staying at home and twirling in my apron while making roast beef and apple pie for a husband anytime soon, so I took the first steady job offered to me. Despite my mother's warnings, I hoped that things would be at least a little different in public school so many decades later.

I started my career mid-year after spending the first two weeks of the semester at the district offices trying to get the paperwork and the signatures straight. This meant I got to hear the substitute who covered for me those first two weeks say to my new students, "I know you are going to miss me, kids, but I am hoping that Ms. Felcher will do as good a job as me." Of course, the kids immediately booed me, and, of course, I noticed her grammar.

    The first year is always legendary for leaving the new teacher shell-shocked. Mine was no different. I was asked to teach all my classes in different classrooms, several of them at the adjacent community college because our school was too packed. Schlepping from class to class across two enormous campuses while laden with books and papers was the easy part of this trial by fire.

    As a first-year teacher, I had to attend meetings with the "mentor" I had been assigned, and we would role-play parent phone calls and teaching situations. She was an English teacher with a whiny high-pitched voice, who punctuated most of what she said with a laugh that seemed to imply an ironic view of things. In fact, she was always earnest, never ironic, and the laugh, irritatingly confusing. "You got the new text book from the lady in the book room? (laugh)" or " You teach in five different classrooms, two of them at the college? (laugh)." When she came in to observe my class, she documented every minute I spent. Her biggest warning? That I not use my sense of humor. No laugh from her that time. In fairness, she did advocate for me to teach in only one room next term.

She and I were not a match, but as a new teacher I was given the time to observe other teachers. I saw teachers whose classes were regimented to the last second and teachers who allowed a free-for-all in their classrooms, while claiming they liked the noise. I saw teachers who lectured without room for discussion or who allowed endless and unfocused discussion. I saw teachers who would shrug and roll their eyes at their students after they ran out of things to say, and I saw teachers who always had clever questions in mind to keep the conversation growing. I saw teachers whose rooms were covered in entertaining and instructive images, which belied the torturous tedium they offered, and I saw teachers whose rooms were a mess, but the kids were in line and on point.

It wasn't until I walked into a classroom filled with kids, many with shaved heads and oversized white t-shirts (the gang style of the day), who were listening so intently to their teacher, that I realized I might have actually found a mentor. The teacher repeated the term he was quizzing, "Synecdoche?"

One of the t-shirted fellows nearly jumped out of his seat to raise his hand, and the teacher responded, "Ok, Mr. _____, you think you have the answer now?"

"Yes, Teacher!"

"Okay, then. . ."

"When you use the *part* for the *whole*; you *know*, like get your butt *over* here or what *you* said, 'All hands on *deck.' Right?*"

"Very good, Mr. _____," said his teacher. With that, the teacher and the class cracked up at his examples, and the student reveled in being right and in amusing his teacher.

The teacher continued with other literary terms and the examples that made the terms understandable and useful. They all wanted to get the right answer and to think of examples on their own. This was my mentor; this was how I was going to teach.

I learned most of what I know from Mr. ___, and if it weren't for him, I might not have gone back for my MA in English. He reinforced my instincts about the idiocy of education classes and relying on the "Teacher Editions" of text books. After all, doctors don't take doctor classes; they study medicine; lawyers, the law. Following that rule, English teachers, should study--ENGLISH! So I did, and it wasn't long before I found ways to dash entirely the increasingly pictorial textbooks from my curriculum. I used the complete texts that I purchased for a dollar a copy or anthologies of texts that hadn't been used in decades in order to get the kids to read and write smartly, rather than look at pictures and answer questions correctly. Not that all these endeavors are diametrically opposed, but the latter does not always lead to the former, that's for sure.

That first year was the first of several first years, all challenging despite my growing experience, but I took from them the lessons that have made me the teacher I am today, and I hope to share them with you here.

ANXIETY...

SCORES WALK IN (8/3)

It's now early August, the Sunday of the year for us school teachers (and probably everyone else who has never quite shaken off the tyranny of school schedules). I have been at this school for eight years and am girding up for reentry, but I am also looking forward to seeing the kids who made the Herculean effort to modify their schedules to sign up for my classes, despite, or I should say because of my reputation as a "challenging" teacher.

I teach AP English Language and Composition and when the scores came out in July, I was pleased to see that of the 24 kids I taught, all took the AP test, and all but two passed. Here is the rub: I will walk into school this fall, proud of my students' accomplishments only to be told "test scores walk into the room."

In the land of test-score accountability, when a teacher generates excellent scores and motivates students to be perhaps a little more excellent than they naturally are, the bureaucrats see the success has having nothing to do with the teacher and everything to do with the student. They all but ignore what in other instances is the all-important "test data."

When I have classes that comprise disruptive students who don't want to make the effort to learn because more compelling things--cell phones, sex, dice, movies, music, gangs, computers, peer acceptance--take up their time, guess whose fault it is when their test scores are below average? Don't those test scores also walk into the room? The fact is, most of my students improve their test scores, but in rooms like the one I describe here, I have to do more than teach. In these classrooms I have to change the culture and instill basic values and "habits of mind" into children who do not understand or have any use for the kind of success I value: a rich life governed by curiosity and a strong, unflappable work ethic, a life where one is never bored and is always growing.

All that said, the message here is as follows: The smart kids walk in smart; therefore, no teacher has any real impact on them. Your 91% pass rate is matter of course, given that you have motivated students, so don't you dare pat yourself on the back. But students who walk into high school with 5th-grade reading levels and no interest in academics, who sleep during class and during standardized tests, who curse out teachers who demand something of them, and who see success only in concrete financial terms usually unrelated to what they are studying (hence their contempt for us "underpaid losers")--their tests scores are all your fault, so take that cat-o-nine-tails and start swinging!

This double-standard is all part of the feel-good, encouraging environment we call public school. Well, at least I still have a little summer time left. . . .

CLAD OR unCLAD? THAT IS THE QUESTION! (8/11)

Three years ago, as a means of earning No Child Left Behind money, the District and the union, once again in bed together and with only money and efficiency in mind, decided that all teachers needed a CLAD credential. I would love to let you in on what this particular acronym stands for, but I can never remember. I do know it has something to do with teaching students for whom English is not a first (or even second or third?) language. I had already been teaching for over 20 years at the time, and I had student-taught and then actually taught ESL (English as a Second Language) for several years--including night school. My ESL students had been known to read and act out scenes from *King Lear* and weep at the end of Kurosawa's *Ran*, yet I now needed this credential in order to teach the students I had been teaching all these years.

I pushed our administration to have someone come to our school to give us veteran teachers the class we needed in order to earn this credential. It turns out, since I had left the District several years earlier to prove my mettle in other schools, and I no longer had the required number of consecutive years in public school, I was ineligible for the class. Instead, I got to watch my colleagues take this free once-a-week class on their way to CLAD proficiency, while I had to make other, more expensive arrangements.

    I was relegated to an online course of study because none of the local universities offered CLAD courses separate from their credential programs. And I would have to pay $2500 of unreimbursed money for this pleasure. There were just no other options, and the administration made it clear that they might be forced to use one's lack of a CLAD to move us around to different schools like chess pieces. So I signed up, bought the $80 book and began the course work that lasted through the spring and summer of that year.

    I wish I could remember the names of the four redundant, mind-numbing courses I took, but I cannot. What the work amounted to was my recounting and describing everything I already do and have been doing in my classes for years: class readings, related outside readings, guided book journals, reader responses designed to help them flesh out and organize their analytical responses to the literature, and culminating analytical essays. The good news is that unlike education classes I have taken in person, where I have had to force myself not to snipe and roll my eyes, I got to sit at a computer far away from my classmates and my instructors.

Oh, what an enthusiastic "sharer" I became. Often the first to post in the online discussions, I restated the obvious with such faux élan I almost believed it myself. When my fellow classmates joined the discussion threads, I would respond to their posts with tail-wagging enthusiasm about their skill and creativity and not make a single comment about their glaring subject/verb or pronoun/antecedent agreement mistakes (one of the instructors could barely negotiate the English language himself!). I created an online persona of the teacher who is always positive and eager.

Occasionally, I would sense the presence of a compatriot, whose contempt for all the patronizing, self-satisfied posts was barely concealed beneath the "Wonderful, ideas, Robyn, but perhaps you should focus a bit on the actual reading of the literature instead of just on the videos and the acting." Or "Wow, I wish I had thought of that, Eugene. It's heartening to see someone so driven by the personal problems of all your students that you provide so many formerly downtrodden guest speakers for them to learn both life lessons and English. But what work are the students actually doing in your classes?"

I would never reveal myself. Only once, when the instructor seemed to grade us completely arbitrarily (especially, since she never clearly explained what she was asking of us and never responded to our work), did I tip my hand a little. Though I was tempted to out her as the fraud she was and was ready to give up on the entire sham in the process, instead (get ready, here come the ed biz terms) I asked her how we were to learn to explain our expectations clearly if she did not "model clear expectations" for us, her humble students.

    She took the bait and spelled things out after that. Would that I had kept my mouth shut and settled for the lesser grade. Now the directions were so explicit you couldn't help but see how stupid the work was:

    Write a lesson plan where you get your students to talk about how important it is that multiple cultures coexist in your school, and use the format on page 72 of your book for this lesson plan. Then use this lesson plan in your own classroom and record its effectiveness."

Uh. . . . nope.

    But I did go to my computer and talk about how "valuable" such a lesson was and how "clear expectations," "scaffolding," and "prior knowledge" played into the students' success, blah, blah, blah.

    The nadir of this experience came when my dad fell ill with lung cancer. I had to sit at the computer in his room as he lay in the bed nearby. I had to take time away from him to respond to all the meaningless drivel. Nonsense for nonsense while life and death were playing out right next to me. It was excruciating, to say the least.

If there is any small silver lining in this grim tale, it is that these abysmal classes marched me up the pay-scale, so I could pay them off sooner. I had been a slow goer on that climb. Courses like "American Poetry: 1945 to the Present" took way more time and energy than the District's salary point offerings like "The Whole World Dances—Let's Learn About Cultures (Note: Bring comfortable shoes and be ready to dance!)." Sure, I know there is a need for these salary-point classes, but not for me.

Despite the salary scale bounce, the CLAD courses did teach me something: I will never get back the time I spent on this dehumanizing experience, and more important, I will never get back the time with my dad or the bits of my soul that I had to use to conjure up a self I hope NEVER to become.

QUALITY OF LIFE? (8/18)

I ended the summer at a party in Santa Monica, and as the sun cast its late afternoon glow on the fluttering blue tablecloths, an autumnal chill reminded me that school was fast approaching.

I perched myself near a dear friend who has worked for 25 years at the liberal arts, forward-thinking Santa Monica private school where I also worked for a few years. When he told me he was already back at school, even though there were two weeks remaining in August, I playfully teased him. Then when he asked me when I get to go back to school, I nearly burst into tears. He saw my sudden distress, took my hand as if to call a truce, and simply said, "It's a quality of life thing, as you know." Right, quality of life. I got it immediately.

I had left that sunny private school because I was offered more money at another private school, and since I had left my original post at a public school and taken a large pay cut for the opportunity to teach at the Santa Monica school in the first place, I could not see refusing what amounted to $8000 more per year and a shorter commute to this other school. I was again at the crossroads between quality of life and quality of pay, the two fundamental aspects of working life that rarely coincide in the teaching profession, if they do anywhere.

I had decided to return to public school because union protections, a stable salary, health benefits, and a retirement package were enticing me once again. But, now that school is about to start, I think it is time to think about my friend's searing reminder, "It's a quality of life thing," once again.

When I go back to school in a couple of weeks, I will face five classes instead of the normal six. I had been warned that the administration would remove my extra class because of cuts. I had taught an extra class every year because I need the money and because teaching the extra class means I do not have any time to cover another teacher's class and manage their behavior problems. I'd have been a sub if I thought I could gracefully handle what other teachers tolerate in their rooms.

I will face an average of 34 students in each of my classes (and I hear these days that this is a luxuriously low number), and these will be English students who can learn only by practice, which means by writing extensively. Most weekends I will face a one or two-foot high stack of paper to read and correct. I will also teach two classes in a local private religious school a couple of afternoons a week, and I will tutor a couple of kids privately because I have turned my life into the Gordian knot faced by many worker bees: my lifestyle ameliorates the effects of hard work, but I need the hard work to afford the lifestyle.

Let me just say that I am working all the time from September to June and the summer thrill of having a real life, of reconnecting with my friends and family for nights at the Hollywood Bowl, for morning dance classes and coffees at The Farmer's Market, for afternoon strolls along Venice beach, and for scenic drives to the lake or to Santa Barbara--I could go on—evaporates with the opening bell.

This is not to say that I did not work hard at

that sunny private school. In fact I might have worked harder there than I do now, but there is that persnickety "quality of life" question again. At that school motivation and hard work were not an issue with either the kids or my colleagues; I taught five classes with 18 kids in each class, if that; and I was given time in the day to grade work, answer and make phone calls, and prepare for class. There was even time to talk meaningfully to other teachers with whom I shared an office between classes.

At that school, if I had to write college recommendations, I got a day off. When grades were due, we all got a day off to write and proofread narrative reports. We enjoyed trips and school holidays and school-wide forums and other thoughtful and inspiring breaks from what in many other schools can be the endless deadening routine. I would often spend evenings and weekends at school, but the work was always a pleasure because despite the physical limitations of the school plant (the school did not enjoy the embarrassment of riches the public school district tends to squander), the atmosphere was open and inviting, the technology current.

I had to meet more frequently with parents, other teachers, administrators, but most were articulate and intelligent. Conversations were usually engaging, even when frustrating, and I got to grow as a teacher, which was as important as the students' growth. But the pay was abysmally low. I guess this is the heart of the "quality of life" question: work in a place that values what you value or work in a place that will pay you well.

At the public school, at the end of a semester we are to give finals and then are expected to grade them and calculate all the students' final grades over night--hence why many teachers opt to show movies instead of give finals. We write hundreds of college recommendations, but on our own time, and usually over the Thanksgiving break. We have to turn in grades every four and a half weeks, but students don't get these grades until a few weeks after they are submitted to the office, so they are already stale by the time parents see them. We are asked to meet with parents, who are sometimes hostile towards teachers, and we are expected to deal with students who have no use for school and whose parents are often too busy to get involved or simply hope the school will serve as a holding pen for their kids.

Most important, because public school teachers can be neither praised nor punished, and administrators often do not have the time or inclination to perform meaningful and stimulating teacher evaluations, teachers are seen essentially as all the same but for our seniority: interchangeable cogs in a machine. Because of logistical constraints, administrators often think nothing of moving teachers and students around from room to room or class to class, sometimes at the last minute just before the start of a semester and sometimes well into the semester; and they expect teachers to adjust to what can feel like seismic shifts without complaint. Sometimes the entire balance of a class is destroyed with the sudden transfer of students, and sometimes teachers have no time to properly prepare for the new classes they have been handed the day before school starts. The only assumption one can make is that the only skill teachers need is the ability to handle what's dealt them by an unwieldy system.

    The meeting rule that all participants are to "Presume positive intentions" is a presumption that does not come naturally in this environment. Sometimes administrators treat teachers as if they have no right to be around the very children they are left alone with from the minute they set foot on the job. It often seems as if it is more important that teachers just put in the time than work hard to improve the quality of the time they put in.

    People often refer to public-school teachers as the "fighters on the front lines" in this daily education "battle," and these metaphors are not funny or coincidental, especially since budget cuts usually prove that teaching positions are not considered as sacrosanct as District sinecures. In addition to the hammering teachers take for test scores and student performance, the subtle and not so subtle messages about how we are valued throw into question why we do what we do, especially when the structure in which we work usually seems so contradictory to the task.

The improved quality of their writing shows that the students learn something in my classroom, and at the end of the year they all thank me for working hard for them and "fighting the good fight"—there's that combat metaphor again. They also return to school long after they graduate to report the joy of their having been excellently prepared for college and life in general. And, yes, all that is "rewarding," the word we use as the ultimate consolation prize for small paychecks.

Unfortunately, as long as a public school system uses NO! more than YES! or expects the worst and demands the mediocre, public school teachers have no choice but to inure themselves to institutional demoralization and take comfort in tenure, benefits, and isolation.

The good news is that public school teachers can still work towards a comfortable retirement. The bad news is that retirement is often short lived because "quality of life" was just not an important enough consideration.

A RETIREE'S VISION (8/24)

    Since weekends and summers are meant to be time well spent, away from the cares of school, it is odd that much of the time I have spent has been with teachers--current and former colleagues, dance teachers, writing teachers, deans, retirees. I guess the job really is in my blood. How embarrassing!
    During the summer I got to spend the day with a woman who taught English with me at my first public school roost almost 25 years earlier, and has long been retired. Since we could never afford

a house in the city, when I re-entered public school for my second stint, my husband and I bought a house in the mountains. My friend had had her house up at the lake her whole life, since it had been her family's mountain home. As we tooled along in our little boat, she reminisced about spending summers working at the small local post office or answering phones and planning her sabbatical at one of the lakeside estates. What a concept--a sabbatical! I have never had an opportunity to even consider the possibility of a sabbatical in my decades long employment as a teacher.

    We also caught up on gossip. My friend is part of a group of retired teachers who attend a luncheon the first day of school each fall semester to celebrate the fact that they no longer have to endure the tyranny of bells, papers, and tedium. She remembered feeling that as an English teacher, particularly one who ran an outstanding newspaper, she was working all the time. She remembered the feeling that the paper work would never end, but she got through it all, which was a hopeful sign for me.

    We laughed at the memory of the interminable "in-services" we withstood at after-school meetings, and I told her of the new ones we still face year after year, all designed to support the theory of the month. These theories always turn into a mantra that is given district-wide importance until the next bout of magical thinking replaces it. Boy, did we have a good laugh.

She remembered the in-service where a "Language Acquisition" expert came in to teach us how to "effectively incorporate vocabulary into our daily lesson plans." This particular in-service required that we participate in ill-conceived vocabulary relay races and other silly games that seemed to me to be antithetical to the design of a rigorous classroom (but then again "Rigor" had not become a magical word yet). As the "expert" spoke, the faculty sat in silence, some surreptitiously and some not so surreptitiously grading papers, doing crosswords, reading books, knitting. I sat roiling in my naiveté.

The presenter suggested we use the word "contesserate" (a word I had never heard before or since, for that matter, at least not as a verb!). She then offered her suggestions for teaching the word: "Have the children 'air write' the new word on their palms and feel how the word sounds on their lips; then have them write all the things they think the word means and go over why they think it means these things."

ALL RIGHT! THAT'S IT!

Despite the warning hands of my friends, pressed firmly into my shoulders to keep me seated and quiet (they knew me and my inability to stay silent at these things), I arose, "DO YOU THINK WE HAVE ALL DAY TO TEACH ONE WORD? AND DO YOU THINK WE ARE IDIOTS?"

At this memory, my friend laughed and laughed. She did not remember a word of the in-service itself, but she did remember this outburst of mine, "DO YOU THINK WE ARE IDIOTS?" and then laughed and laughed again at how obtuse I must have been not to realize that that was exactly what the "experts" think of teachers. She wondered how I could not know that such a misuse of our time was to be expected and my not taking it in stride was a waste of valuable personal energy.

Meanwhile, I still fume at the notion that these "experts" who have opted out of the classroom think it is okay to spread the gospel of excellent teaching tactics to those of us doltish enough to continue the struggle. What adds to the fire is that these presenters rarely show any evidence of their own skill as they mangle the English language themselves.

In one instance, after a series of budget twists, our own "literacy expert" was cut, and in my sympathy for her--she was one who cared deeply and had the smarts to make her work effective--I worked hard to get her a job I knew of at a local private school. Though she said she would take the job when it was offered, she waited most of the summer before realizing that she should not take the job because actually getting back into teaching, prepping, grading, classroom managing felt like just too much for her. Hmm, what does that tell you?

My friend and I then spoke of another in-service the time the magical term was "Backwards Planning." After she and I finished roaring at the name of this ingenious strategy, I told her what I thought it meant: Focus and clarify your teaching goal first, then carefully plan accordingly all the steps you need to get there. She broke up again, and said, "Isn't that just PLANNING?" Ah, once again the obvious stated obviously.

After our day on the lake and a leisurely dinner, I asked her how she survived such a lengthy career in the school district. She said, "I remember only the good times." I looked at her puzzled, and she continued "Well, the time with friends, of course, but really the time in class with the kids."

That's the right answer.

SEPARATION ANXIETY? (8/31)

Just as the year is about to start a friend of mine decides to resign from the LAUSD. In addition to being an excellent science teacher, she is a licensed personal trainer and fitness expert who did the math and realized that working part-time in her field would pay more than what she would earn as a teacher.

She had initially aimed to go part time, but when she looked at her incoming student rosters and realized that because of budget constraints she would have more students than she did when she taught full time--for much less pay—that was it. Wellness Spa, soothing fountains, and soft voices, here she comes.

She said she thinks of the job the way one thinks about relationships. Would she stay with a man who exploited or abused her? Good point. So why stay in a job that demands she work hard and suffer certain indignities for pay that would barely cover living expenses.

The funniest and saddest part of my friend's resignation is her having to fill out the District's "Confidential Separation Questionnaire," which is a checklist of possible reasons for the decision to "separate." Here are some of the best:

Paperwork/record keeping
Too many duties in general

Take home work
Too many non-teaching related duties
Many meetings
Unmotivated students
Unsupportive parents
Student discipline policy
Personal safety concerns at school site
Lack of support from administrator in general. . .
Communication flow at school. . .
Salary. . . .
District's policies and/or goals
Lack of input into school policies
Lack of input into curriculum. . .
And my personal favorite. . SIMPLY TIRED OF WORKING!

One has to ask why these common District working conditions are examined only when one is ready to quit? Does it seem strange that the District, test purveyors extraordinaire, cannot seem to get this one test right, given that the BEST answer is not CIRCLE THE MOST IMPORTANT REASON but ALL OF THE ABOVE!

Perhaps if there were genuine concern about these conditions, which are so obvious and pervasive that they are printed on this form, the District would not lose so many of their good young teachers. Adios and best wishes to my friend, I say!

REALITY...

DAY 1 (9/9)

The new school year hits most of us hard. Some new teachers are digging out from under the dusty remnants of the 30-year careers of retired teachers. Others are grappling with a gross lack of technical support--no copiers, no internet, no keys. Still others are overwhelmed and disheartened by the enormous class sizes. Teaching positions have evaporated, but the students have not, and we who remain now take up the slack--more students packing fewer classes. More work for teachers, less pay.

For me it is no surprise to see I am facing the continuing decline of standards, no matter how many "standards" we write on the board when evaluators come into our rooms, and no matter how well the students can report which standards they are learning. Once again, I have an AP Literature class full of students who have read not a page, not a line this summer even though there was assigned summer reading. Their essays are devoid of shape, thinking, purpose, and many took an AP Language class last year only to fail the AP test. Yet I would bet those who failed the test earned A's, B's, maybe C's, in their AP classes.

This institutionally sanctioned disconnect--AP access for everyone despite their basic skills and mild work ethic--makes the job very difficult, A couple of students actually are ready for AP, so here is the quandary: do I turn the class into the basic class most of the students seem to need or do I leave the majority in the dust and focus on the few advanced students?

In all, this chaotic first day was particularly bad for me mostly because I wore closed toe shoes for the first time in two months and had to run around the campus with swollen feet on the hunt for paper and working copiers. Experience tells me that the chaos will subside, only to be supplanted by the routine, signified by the ringing of bells.

Just as in *Hamlet* it's not the action but the thought between the actions that matters, I have to remember it's not the bells that matter, but the learning that happens between the bells.

WHAT IS "ACCESS" ANYWAY? (9/10)

I hand out an Anthony Lane *New Yorker* essay about the Beijing Olympics Opening Ceremony and ask the same question that I am certain all Advanced Placement English Language teachers ask their students: "What is the tone of this piece?" Of course, Lane, typically astute and ready to debunk, warns us not to be so enamored of the aesthetics of fascism, which seemed to have governed that elaborate opening ceremony, down to the young singer replaced because she was not pretty enough. Unfortunately, many of the students, programmed not to question what they read and who are uncomfortable doing much more than decoding, did not get it.

The class is full of students who had taken some class over the summer specifically designed to ready them for this "college-level English course." Instead of reading the E.B. White essays I had assigned as AP summer reading, which might have readied them for Lane's piece, they report that their summer-school teacher read aloud Fitzgerald's *The Great Gatsby* word by word and they did no writing or reading on their own. Of course, you have to take what kids say with a grain of salt, but it is obvious that these kids are either not prepared or not willing to be independent critical readers.

When I ask these students whether they know

what I mean by tone or what a thesis is or whether they have ever used college manuscript format, they blanch and run to their counselors to switch out of the class.

What I had considered basic questions turn out to be too daunting, and that exodus leaves me with nine students in the class. Although at my school some Art History field-trip classes have similarly low numbers, in English classes this low number is considered a scourge because of the impact such a low number has on the other English classes.

At least by the end of the year all nine would pass the test, and of the eleven 5's the school's 149 AP students earned, five of them would be my students. But even though the class was a joy for the nine students who remained and for me as a teacher, the administrators demanded that such small English classes never happen again (unless it's Art History, I guess).

Back to the exodus. . . I am aware that there are lots of reasons students are not prepared for college-level work. The issue at the heart of this situation is this question of access to higher-level classes. Administrators insist the test scores do not matter as much as how many kids enroll into the classes and take the test.

This goal is the kind of stuff they make all those feel good school movies about: students without any interest in school, who would rather taunt the teacher and one another than learn anything, often break out into song when they hit milestones, then get the best scores in history on their culminating exams. Who wouldn't be heartened by such stories and motivated to join Teach for America, so they too could enjoy that change the world feeling (if only for a year or two, until they discover more serious and lucrative careers).

I tend to think that giving access to ill-prepared students is like giving access to the deep end of a swimming pool to non-swimmers. Would I take AP Calculus if I tremble at simple math? Why, then, would students take AP English if they don't read regularly or intelligently? Why would we set them up to drown?

Usually students take AP classes because they have done well in their previous classes or they behaved well enough to prove their motivation. That behavior should certainly be rewarded and often those students do manage in AP classes. But to change the high-level courses to courses designed to accommodate and remediate low skills seems to fly in the face of a standards-driven education. Why is there a test at the end of an AP course if it doesn't matter? And why doesn't their failure on this AP test matter?

I wholeheartedly believe everyone should

have access to all high-level classes, but that access begins *way* before one gets to the upper grades where these classes are usually taught. Access begins in elementary and middle school, and if not then, at the very least in 9th grade. My students tend to do well on national tests like the AP test. I usually teach them for a couple of years in a row, so they get lots of practice reading and writing analytically. If all students were asked to do AP-level work from the minute they enter high-school—in other words, if they were all acclimated to the water *before* diving into the deep end of the pool--then the dream of high enrollment could be achieved, and high enrollment and high test scores wouldn't have to be an either/or choice.

SELECTING AP TEACHERS—WHO DECIDES AND HOW? (9/11)

Last spring department chairs, Advanced Placement teachers, and administrators stayed late one evening to codify the requirements for selection of AP teachers. Since the College Board started to notice great disparity between student grades and scores on the national exam, AP teachers have been asked to submit syllabi and course work to be audited by the Board to ensure the work meets the prescribed goals of the class. Passing this audit is the first requirement, but the school needed to come up with its own criteria for teacher selection.

The first four criteria received the majority of the votes:

1. Percentage of a teacher's students who take the AP test at the end of the term
2. Formal training with the College Board
3. Teaching experience (in particular, teaching AP)
4. Higher degrees like an MA or PhD

The following criteria were suggested but did not receive the highest votes:

5. Pass Rate on the AP exam
6. College teaching experience
7. Student evaluations

The final criterion, though suggested, did not receive any votes:

    8. Rotating AP classes among several teachers

When I asked my students--our clientele-- to vote on these same eight criteria, they picked the following:

    1. AP teaching experience
    2. College teaching experience
    3. Higher degrees
    4. Student Evaluations

The students felt pass rates were important but not as important as the first four. What they rated dead last were "the percentage of students who take the test" and "rotation among teachers." They felt it should be a given that students who take the time to take an AP class take the AP test and that rotating the course among several teachers was inconsistent with the teaching experience requirements.

    The issues surrounding the AP teacher selection process are in keeping with the problems of "access" in general, but now we are talking about teacher access. So after all the talk about criteria, "Rotation among teachers" won the day. We maintained the status quo.

    Usually teachers who rely on the AP label to prove their worth as teachers instead prove that allowing all teachers "access" to AP, while good for teachers, might not be so good for students. The irony is that the excellent teachers with whom I have worked do not need to teach AP courses to know they do excellent work. They teach every course with the same curiosity, intelligence, enthusiasm, and rigor to ensure that their students who might want access to higher-level classes will not drown in the deep end.

ONE WEEK DOWN—THIRTY-NINE TO GO... (9/12)

At the start of every year, most English teachers have to handle students who would rather interpolate than interpret; who settle for translation rather than analysis; who offer repetitive reporting instead of the conscious shaping of an argument. Fortunately, critical thinking is a teachable skill and experience dictates that once the students' eyes open to the workings of figurative language, we can build from there.

Naturally, I warn all my students of the rigors ahead, and naturally, upon hearing my warnings, several run to their counselors bubbling and blathering that they need a "better" teacher or a lower-level class. When the counselors tell me not to "scare the students away," I have to shake my head. My goal is to help students learn to think, read, and write, critically and analytically. Learning is scary in the same way that the truth hurts: both demand action, and we may or may not be ready to take that action. If the students choose not to face the challenge, I cannot change that.

I remember calling a parent last year after a girl left my honors class for a basic class so she could be with her friends (let's just say they were girls with more social than academic interests).

This girl was academically up to the AP challenge and should not have switched, but her mother said, "She needs a social life too." Who am I to argue?

Now that my classes are settling down and the students' needs have clarified my goals, I myself need a social life too. A daily Scrabble move in the endless tournament I am playing with my high-school pal might not cut it. I also need to figure out how to cut my workload but still give kids enough practice to move them ahead. Having 39 or 40 students in an English class is untenable. The truth hurts, all right.

I must say that I do marvel at those few teachers whose classes must also be overloaded in this the current climate, but who manage to leave school everyday at 3pm sharp with only a cell-phone in their hands. I guess my truth demands a bit more action.

SUMMON(S)ED BY A HIGHER POWER? (9/28)

We are starting the fourth week of school and students are still changing their classes and adjusting their schedules because there are five weeks built into the start of every term for them and their counselors to get it right (What does that say about what's being taught in the first quarter of the term, you might ask? Not my bailiwick, so I'm not saying *any*thing).

Part of the chaos of students' switching from class to class comes in the form of student "teacher assistants" bringing around little yellow papers called "summonses" for kids to meet with their counselors or various other administrators around the campus. The kids are not "summoned" to these offices; nope, they are "summonsed," a word that connotes something far more important than just being called to an office.

My Shakespeare class erupts into laughter when there is a seventh knock at the door. We have been reviewing the first scene of *Hamlet* and discussing the meaning and function of the first words "Who's there?" It's a line that some would argue sets the tone of the play. Of course, this knock means yet another teaching assistant bearing yet another summons. One of my students has go to the office in order to receive his locker number.

Out the boy goes, far across the campus to the main office, and then back he comes. When he returns twenty minutes later, I ask whether he has solved his locker problem.

"Uh, well, no . . . This was a summons for them to tell me that they are going to summons me again later today because they did not have a locker available now."

Fortunately, it's early enough in the semester for me to summon up my sense of humor.

IT STARTED WITH A GIGGLE.... (10/12)

It starts with a giggle that moves around the room quickly. My students are in the midst of some "low-stakes," District-sanctioned test, so I stop typing the departmental e-mail that I know my colleagues will delete before reading to ask the kids what's so funny.

The response: "This question asks us to choose the best meaning for the phrase, 'Susie suddenly stopped dead in her tracks' and here is one of the choices: A) Susie was walking, then she died suddenly.'"

The class collapses into laughter again. Two more hours of their time wasted taking these ridiculous departmental "benchmark" tests contracted to and developed by some professional testing company. The students are asked to read brief essays, personal letters, cartoons, and graphs, but the texts are not textured enough to be effectively analyzed. They are ostensibly about controversial student-oriented topics like cell phone use, video games, obesity, or smoking, but all are constructed as patronizing life messages, which the students must read, analyze, and write about persuasively. If these topics are controversial, one would never know it. The students are asked to discuss the "counterclaim" in each text, but since the stuff is so biased, no clear counterclaim exists--

obesity, smoking, video games are bad and that's that.

Once there were two "best" choices in the multiple choice answers; once not even one of the multiple choice answers applied to the question. Then when we examine this "test data" as a department, we are issued additional "assessment criteria," crafted as a response to the way the students addressed the test questions. If the questions and answers are so poorly constructed that the rubrics have to be modified after the exam is administered, how accurate can the assessment be? The results are only as good as the instrument, and this instrument seems flawed at best.

For the literature component of this test, and I use that term loosely, students have to answer questions related to a story about a village in some place a tad more exotic than their own suburban Los Angeles neighborhoods. The narrator repeatedly describes the respect paid to "Grandfather." Since the kids did not know that a custom in some small villages is to call all the elders "Grandfather," they assume that the narrator is talking about his own grandfather, so they answer about half the questions incorrectly.

One student brings her test up to me to ask what to do in the instance where the answers are listed A), B), D), C). Should she write D for the third answer which should have been marked C but is listed here as D? Now there's a quandary for a kid who wants to get it right.

Not only will my students be judged on their performance on these tests, but according to the DATA battle cry, my credibility as a teacher will also be determined by this data. I am all for accountability, but who's going to be judging and what criteria will they use?

I never teach to any test, particularly any test that requires I water down the curriculum. When my 10th graders were reading *Macbeth* in the context of excerpts of R.D. Laing's *Divided Self*, they were somewhat taken aback when they had to write an essay on the California Exit Exam that asked them to defend the kind of animal they thought best for children—dogs or cats. One of my favorite kids wrote her essay about the Komodo dragon. Perfect!

Most teachers would agree that teaching to any test is the most shortsighted approach to teaching, yet this is the approach that is championed by the District. Reducing teacher accountability to such test data is exactly that: reducing teacher accountability, period.

EVALUATING THE EVALUATORS (10/18)

The people who advocate evaluating teachers based on test scores believe that teaching is a skill that can be judged objectively with the right objective tool. However, most classroom teachers know this is more institutional speak than the best approach. Tests can be one measure, but certainly not the only measure. Perhaps even more important, this test-accountability issue underscores the harried approach to evaluation that prevails in most schools.

Because I see value in teacher evaluation, if done thoughtfully rather than punitively, the first day of the semester I gave the members of my department a teacher self-evaluation I had gleaned from a variety of sources.

The evaluation was based on the teacher's knowledge of his or her subject because without that knowledge the rest of the characteristics evaluated would be impossible to master.

Most public school evaluations usually ask questions like these:

1. Are the students "on task"?

2. Are the students aware of the specific standards they are being taught? Has the teacher posted that standard on the board or indicated it in another way? (It is presumed by those in charge that if a student knows which standard is being taught, then the student will learn that standard. However, several standards at once are usually interwoven into lessons, activities, and assignments, so knowing the standard does not necessarily lead to mastery of anything other than tedium.)

3. Does the teacher perform bureaucratic duties (grading, attending meetings, taking video tests on child abuse and blood pathogens, to name a few) in a timely fashion?

4. Does the teacher sign in (which seems to be the only method for determining whether we show up to school on time)?
5. Is the teacher collegial?
6. Does the teacher show evidence of teaching strategies like "scaffolding" and "backwards planning" and "vertical teaming"? (How's that for institutional thinking?)

The focus on "how" we teach seems to outweigh any look at what we teach or why we teach what we teach. If all we care about is "how" one teaches, we should also notice another how: how low that sets the bar.

(IN)ADEQUATE (10/20)

Some of the teachers I have worked with over the years have the capability of high-powered administrative assistants--they are organized, they know how to read, they usually know their grammar, and they can manage bureaucratic requirements effectively. This is not to cast aspersions on administrative assistants. God knows, they are often more valued and make much more money than teachers. But it is to say that that this skill set is only part of what a high school teacher, particularly an English teacher, needs.

Teachers are often required to limit themselves to the directives and the habits of mind ingrained in them by the bureaucracies in which they work. It seems as if some schools hire people they do not trust to do the job they have been hired to do and construct all kinds of "support" designed to get all teachers to march in sync and tighten the cracks into which they might otherwise fall.

Yes, it's true that the very worst teachers give all teachers a bad name, but the danger lies not in the worst teachers bringing down the reputation of the rest of the teachers; it lies in the best teachers being brought down by the merely adequate.

Just as there is no room for simply adequate surgeons, if teaching is "the most important profession" as I have heard it described, then there is no room for simply adequate teachers. Excellence should be the only option.

But evaluating excellence is problematical because excellence lies in the art of teaching, which is impossible to objectively quantify. Here are some of the elements of the art of teaching:

- the art of knowing and responding to what his/her individual students need
- the art of knowing more than the student at all times and not being afraid to ask questions if he/she does not
- the art of being a lifetime learner
- the art of being able both to improvise and stay on track
- the art of balancing humor with "gravitas" or rigor
- the art of sticking to a mission that both includes the curriculum and maintains a clear and solid moral imperative (by this I mean always keeping in mind why we teach, presuming it's not just to lord it over kids or salve our egos as we hear ourselves speak or as we get kids to say what we want them to say)
- the art of listening creatively so that the students can see themselves in a better light than the light they originally tried to shed on a subject
- the art of meeting students where they are

when they walk into the classroom and in turn getting them well past where they started
• the art of making all students feel safe and potentially successful even when they are struggling
• the art of motivating students from the core rather than just from their reflexes--getting them to want to learn rather than simply fear the test
• the art of getting students to analyze, synthesize, and extrapolate rather than "rinse and repeat."

While some administrators get it, many have been rewarded with promotions either to get them out of the classroom and out of harm's way or for capably maintaining the status quo (we call this demoting up). And these formerly adequate teachers are given the task of evaluating the very qualities that might have eluded them in their own teaching practice.

The sad truth is that a "good" evaluation usually translates to a teacher's passing with a C, but for today's issues, sorry to say, a C is just not good enough. An Austrian friend of mine once described the philosophy when he went to school: A is God; B is teacher; C is student. Using his example, if "C is teacher," then D is student, and we can't afford D's and F's on both sides of the desk.

THERE'S NO BIZ LIKE ED BIZ (10/25)

People often urge the youth of America to become teachers--a noble request, we can agree. But frankly, why should they?

We have all talked about the degradation and demoralization that students and teachers suffer in a system that can neither praise nor punish its teachers. In past essays I have discussed the need for excellent teachers and effective evaluation procedures, and I have discussed both myriad reasons the system seems to be failing and myriad ways to make the public schools actually more effective. But a topic that really needs attention is teacher preparation, which is one of the reasons, if not the key reason, that school districts like mine 1) decided they have to make standardized testing the barometer for success and 2) decided they have to spend time and money to create stringent rules and scripts for teachers, many of whom they never should have hired in the first place.

    A couple of years ago I was asked to guide a student teacher. While most student-teachers enter the room with shiny, motivational posters, big-giant Post-its, ambitious "fun" games, and other "dazzling" (at least they think so) appurtenances, this teacher was of a different breed altogether. He offered none of the glitz; in fact, he offered nothing at all. He had no interest in reading, in thinking, in answering questions, in grading papers, in instructing or in motivating kids, and he made no bones about saying so. All he wanted was to stage-manage school productions and his motivation was in his words "to get paid a full salary and have the kids do all the work." All that mundane classroom stuff? Not for him.

    I spent the first part of the term sitting quietly in a corner of my classroom, like a lunatic cutting out strings of paper dolls from the manila folders he asked for but never used as he stood in front of the room unable to get the attention of the 30 kids in his care. He would clear his throat and stare myopically into the crowd of kids as they were checking phones, talking amongst themselves, or heckling him. I cut away person after person in an 11-inch manila chain, so I would not cause him physical harm as he wasted my students' and, of course, my time.

Now, you might ask, why did I not eject him instantly? Since I have always thought that if I could teach, anyone could teach, I believed I would simply confer with him after each class, and he would start to see the light and improve. Soon, however, the proverbial handwriting was on the wall, or maybe I should say the angry graffiti: HE JUST DOESN"T GIVE A $%&*!

This fellow knew that once he slipped past this silly student-teacher requirement, he would be given a key, a classroom, a bunch of students who would never complain about learning nothing, and best of all, no one would have the time or inclination to observe him. Stay quiet, keep your head down, and health insurance, summers off, and job-security would be his.

After several weeks of reviewing his performance with him and realizing that I would never slice through his apathy, I forwarded my evaluation to his supervisors and mine. I am sure no one will be surprised to learn that no one counseled him out of the profession or failed him in his student-teaching course before more harm could be done. Instead, my students languished until I hammered enough at the process for the administrators to remove him, at least, from my classroom.

But, you ask yourselves, was he eventually removed from his "teacher-education" program? Is money green? He was given another lead teacher and actually "passed" the student-teaching requirement of his education program, though his methods, as he was proud to tell me when he saw me again some time later, remained the same. I guess he showed me!

I was reminded of another equally disheartening incident. Several years ago, a few graduate Education students were enrolled in a couple of the graduate English classes I was taking. What these students all had in common was that they never did the reading and never had anything to say in class. Well into the semester many of them simply dropped the courses. Lo and behold, a year later at my graduation, there they proudly stood under the GRADUATE SCHOOL OF EDUCATION banner. I guess they showed me!

What all these education students showed everyone is what all parents, teachers, retired lawyers, failed doctors, and empty-nest housewives or husbands all know: ANYONE CAN TEACH. But should they?

LA DOLCE VITA (11/3)

This year, as I had predicted, I lost the extra class I had taught for the last nine years, and though this class added the stress of an extra preparation and the attendant papers, it also padded my wallet, which made it a little easier for me to inure myself to teaching four one-and-a-half-hour classes each day with only two brief breaks (20 and

30 minutes respectively). Gates and locks define the boundaries of the campus and these gates and locks are not to be opened until the school day ends, so this means that for the last nine years, I have been almost literally chained to my desk.

Not once in nine years have I ever "met a friend for lunch" or gone off campus to "grab a bite" the way people in grown-up jobs do. Since there is really no time to do anything but teach my classes, answer student questions, and make small talk in the bathroom line, I practically live in my classroom. I have packed my little island with the essential modern conveniences like a fridge stocked with berries, Greek yogurt, organic peanut butter, whole grain bread, cheese, water, juice; a kettle to boil water for my coffee and oatmeal; and my phone, so I can enjoy at least the promise of some contact with the outside world during those two breaks. A colleague of mine once asked whether I was hiding a Murphy bed in my book closet. Hmmm, not a bad idea.

On my way back to class during one of the morning breaks, I got a call from a friend who asked what I was doing for lunch. The question, alive with the thrill of leisure and adulthood, caught me off guard. I paused for a minute and remembered that this year, because I lost my auxiliary class, I am actually free for a significant chunk of two out of three afternoons a week, and this was going to be one of those afternoons. So at 1:15 PM, during the lunch period, I did the previously unimaginable . . . I walked out of school "to meet a friend for lunch," to "grab a bite." Fortunately for me, Dolce Isola had opened its doors just up the street.

  The bright red building with its red and white striped awning and little ice-cream tables and chairs in front stands out like an oasis on an otherwise gray section of south Robertson Boulevard, where I teach. Their pastry case does not contain wilted tuna sandwiches on soggy wheat bread or Brillo pad coffee cake, the normal District lunchroom fare. This case is full of delectable treats like Earthquake chocolate cookies, red velvet cupcakes topped with cream cheese icing, lemon squares, chocolate croissants, tea scones, chocolate truffle torts. I hear the tart tartin is the best anywhere. Just looking at the display case gave me a sense of well-being.

  For lunch my friend and I first shared the homemade guacamole filled with large chunks of avocado and fresh homemade tortillas--hot and satisfying. My friend opted for the Dolce Club Sandwich, and I picked the Ivy Buffet: Normandy chicken salad, fresh tuna salad, pasta a la checca, and lo scogglio potato salad. Every bite delicious, particularly the potato salad, which, to my great joy, was true Mediterranean comfort food, doused in olive oil.

What is perhaps most exciting about Dolce Isola is the fact that it is the bakery for an exclusive uptown restaurant. That means not only had I been sprung from my work confinement for the first time in nine years, and not only had I the chance to spend time with my dear friend, but I also had been enjoying a meal that was being similarly enjoyed in the far tonier reaches of the same boulevard. I had briefly traded my work island for the Dolce Isola and enjoyed every second of it--except I forgot to get dessert!

FINGER-LICKIN' OBNOXIOUS (11/11)

The administration decided to host an assembly for seniors to inform them of important policies and requirements for graduation and other "fun" senior events, ranging from BBQs to prom to the graduation ceremony itself. Teachers were asked to escort their classes to our state-of-the-art auditorium to ensure order, well, theoretically at least.

I scanned the room and saw about six hundred students, five teachers, and two or three administrators. Oh yeah, I knew this would be bad. Knowing my inability to cope with the boorish behavior of masses of students empowered by their anonymity, I dug into my seat, kept my nose in the papers I brought to grade, and the corner of my eye on my own class.

No matter who stood up to speak to the assembly, the din never stopped. The man from Jostens, or whichever cap, gown, and ring company he represented, tried to impart information the kids would need should they make it to the finish line, but only a few listened to him. The poor man had to say, "Listen up, people" as an introduction to almost every phrase he uttered. Remarkably, he never lost his patience.

Then the phelgmatic student-body president

mumbled a request for the students to purchase senior sweatshirts that they loudly considered too pricey, and an assistant principal spoke about what many considered the unreasonable senior attendance policy (7 absences max? Really, that's unreasonable?). Soon the din became an uproar.

I continued to mark comma splices and agreement problems and read and reread the sentences before me in an effort to tune out the noise. The last thing I wanted to do was confront misbehaving students whom I do not know by name.

Finally, after questions no one heard and after an administrator left the stage for lack of stamina; after hoots, hollers, and whistles every time some well-meaning adult called them the Class of 2010; after rude call-outs and continuous inattention to the front of the room, the nightmare ended. Inches from a clean getaway, I rose to lead my students out of the auditorium.

Then I saw them. Two girls in the seats right behind my class were sucking on fried chicken wings, fingers covered in grease. I was nothing short of aghast. Now, I have been known to hunker down over a little KFC myself, much to the dismay of my politically and dietarily savvy friends, but here in this sacrosanct auditorium designed for the top-notch performers who attend this school, food is an absolute no-no.

So I thought about it for a few seconds: do I say something and face inevitable resistance and hostility or do I just ignore this egregious defiance in front of all the students who know I have seen this display and count on me, as one of the adults in this barely controlled chaos, to maintain some form of order?

"Are you *really* eating in here? You have to put that away!" I registered my protest and insisted they modify their behavior. Very teacherly, but I knew I was in for it.

Blank stares. Lips wrapped around wings.

"Put the chicken away!" I remained firm.

"Where?" Finger licks, bone gnawing.

"Wherever you got it from!"

"Hunh?"

"Take out whatever the chicken came in and put it away. NOW!"

"Put it in what? What are you talking about?"

The conversation was so unprofitable, so impossible that I was getting angry at myself for starting it, for wasting my time, and for feeling bad that I didn't have a piece of chicken myself. But I am the adult here, or so they tell me. So why do I feel that sick feeling I always get when I know what the right behavior should be and am made to feel the fool when I try to enforce it.

I turned away from the offenders, cursed heartily under my breath, and muttered that I was just tired of the pigs at this school.

One of the girls says, "DID YOU JUST CALL ME A PIG?!"

Righteous indignation, of all the deflecting nerve!

Before I could say, Original Recipe, all the anger I had worked so hard to quell for that hour and a half of patent, auditorium-wide disrespect rose up in me, and I just let it fly: "I said members of this student body act like a bunch of disgusting pigs, and if you think you fit that description, then YES, I guess I called YOU a pig! Your behavior is a disgrace, an intolerable disgrace, and I am just sick to death of bad behavior!" I turned on my heel and stormed out of the room, muttering to myself like the crazy person I suddenly was.

The question all this raises in me is why anyone would expect any adult to be at the mercy of disrespectful teenagers, who rarely face real consequences for their actions, and NOT get angry. One of my colleagues was recently called a bitch by one of her students, a curse to which she responded in equally colloquial and insulting language. This teacher was not only called out for her behavior by the administration, but she was told that a student's calling a teacher a bitch is not an offense worthy of suspension. Really? Now if the same kid had called one of the administrators a bitch, or dare I say something worse, would that have been an offense worthy of suspension?

I also wonder whether it is just a coincidence that when I cannot get the group of boys who play a wild football game in front of my bungalow classroom (where they are forbidden to play) to stop playing that this teacher, the one called "Bitch," is the ONLY teacher who can get the kids to stop. Fire with fire, I say, unless of course, we suddenly turn this terrible tide and make civil student behavior priority one. Not likely, I fear.

Well, all this contemplation is making me hungry. I think I'll go out and get a little of the finger-licking good stuff and be done with it.

"THE THOUSAND NATURAL SHOCKS THAT FLESH IS HEIR TO" (12/17)

Over the years I have had my share of classroom catastrophes: a boy once threw a stapler at me because he did not like his grade; another tossed a chair because I would not tolerate some behavior that I now cannot remember. Yet another boy came to my summer-school classroom door, one hand on his hip the other arm high, his hand gripping the door frame, body atilt. He greeted me with sleepy eyes and a sly grin, then promptly slid down the door frame to the floor in a druggy heap. Another boy suffered from such intense hypo? hyper? or some other sort of glycemia that his head would suddenly drop down onto the desk and.... lights out. The first time this happened, I myself nearly passed out, but the kids knew exactly what to do and mobilized instantly; one to the cafeteria for orange juice; the other to the restroom for a cool paper towel.

But there are other kinds of classroom catastrophes that usually require the application of some sort of mysterious, institutional red sawdust. Girls usually know to run from the room should illness suddenly hit them, but the boys seem to be less adept at that kind of multitasking. They tend to be paralyzed by their distress, unable to move. One boy, after a breakfast of orange juice and pineapple slices (hmm, was the battery acid canister empty that morning?) suddenly flew to the front of the room, paused, planted his feet, and threw up a stew of orange doused pineapple chunks right next to my desk. The rest of the kids, disgusted and on the verge of losing it themselves, squeezed into a corner of the room as if the mess were going to coagulate into some sort of man-eating blob.

    Once another boy who had eaten only chocolate the entire day decided to stand rooted at my desk, bend slightly forward and dribble saliva, while tepidly claiming he was going to be sick. I got that trash can under his face not a moment too soon to receive the chocolate stream that emanated from his nose and mouth. And I used to like chocolate! (Ah, who am I kidding, I still like it! Takes more than that to frighten me away).

    Several years ago, I had a student who suffered from many learning challenges but was mainstreamed anyway (no pun intended, or maybe there is, you decide). I was teaching a 10th-grade honors English class, where the kids had been mostly uninterested in anything I had to say, but during this particular class, they were riveted. I was going on and on about Macbeth and the Wyrd sisters as I was pushing them to contemplate the statement, "Nothing is but what is not." They burned their eyes into me, sealed their mouths shut, and honed their attention. I went on and on because I knew I had them now. Yup, they were getting it at last. After the bell, they filed out silently, and I was awestruck. I was good, but I had no idea that I was THAT good. What a day!

After the class I was about to grab a bite of lunch. . .

. . .when a student, who had come into the room after the class to work through lunch, as kids often did, asked me whether someone had peed on the floor. Peed? I whipped around and saw what looked like apple juice puddled in a chair and on the floor beneath that chair and thought, NO, NO WAY, NO ONE PEED, THAT'S JUST . . Wait a minute. . . Then I remembered who had been sitting there. Though I did not perform a taste test, I knew it had to be my learning-challenged student since that had been her seat. But I had no idea how or why or when this could have happened. Then some of the other students from that class came back into the room with their lunch in tow, and I tried my best to be delicate when I asked whether they had "noticed anything during class."

"NOTICED ANYTHING?" one girl replied. "ARE YOU KIDDING, ME? NOTICED ANYTHING?" She went on. . . _____started peeing in her chair about 15 minutes into the class, and we were all staring at you to try to get you to see what was happening and to do something about it. But NOOOOOOO, you just went on and on and on, Macbeth this; Macbeth that; nothing is nothing is nothing, blah blah blah."

Well, I laughed so hard, I almost. . . .

THE SUBLIME TO THE DELICIOUS (2/6)

As I have been known to confess to those close to me, when it comes to sweets, I am an unabashed purveyor of the pedestrian. Most people who have been to a Ralph's Supermarket in my city have probably noticed the bakery section with its apple turnovers, banana muffins, red-velvet cupcakes, entire cakes, even half cakes—presumably to add variety for the discriminating tastes waiting at home. Whatever glutinous confection you have a hankering for you can pretty much find in this section of the store, right in front of you, the minute you walk in. Since I am stuck with the kind of willpower that needs constant reviving and have been unable to resist many of these offerings in the past, I try to enter the store at the other end, where the fruit is colorfully and bountifully ensconced. But to no avail.

Unfortunately, one item in that dreaded bakery always summons me: chocolate donuts. Clamshells with a twelve-count sit stacked on the bakery tables, neat rows of the taunting chocolate visible through the plastic. Only $4.99 for the Ralph's Club member. How can one resist? Don't they contain all the food groups, milk, eggs, flour, and cocoa (yes, I count cocoa as a food group)?

One of these perfectly round donuts and a

glass of milk means instant transport to childhood. The chocolate coating cracks a bit as your teeth sink into it, and the edges of the fresh golden cake beneath break away first. Then you're left with a thick knot of cake and chocolate at the center, one perfect bite.

So I'm in my kitchen, eating over the sink like a single person. The first bite breaks the donut into the expected pieces, edges first, then the center, and I punctuate each bite with a gulp of milk. As I stand there in a chocolate reverie, for the first time, I actually scrutinize the clamshell container the way one, still warm with sleep, reads the cereal box over and over again when chomping on breakfast flakes.

I had never really looked at the label before because I usually rip it to pieces in my eagerness to break in and grab the goodies. Plus, looking too closely at the label would encourage the kind of food shaming that would put a damper on the whole experience. But this time, since I must have been a tad more delicate, the label, still in tact, reads, "Chocolate Enrobed Donuts." ENROBED! Not chocolate covered, but "enrobed"? Really? Chocolate ENROBED Donuts? I couldn't get over it.

I had been teaching Beowulf and there's that moment in my translation where Wiglaf, Beowulf's protégé, claims he would rather be "robed" in the deadly flames of the dragon than abandon his leader in his hour of need. The image of Wiglaf bravely and ceremoniously enrobed in flames moved me. I had to wonder, did the labeler mean to equate the thick cover of chocolate with vestments, used for clerical ceremonies, as the word enrobed implies? Did the labeler also see these donuts as the source of some kind of religious experience, not just your everyday snack? Who would have expected a grocery store label to contain the perfect metaphor? Who would have expected the ridiculous to be so sublime.

TEST–SCORE TYRANNY (3/6)

I once suggested the teachers in my department read one another's Shakespeare essays and after assessing them together, we could give an award for the best of the essays. According to reading lists I had generated from my colleagues the previous year, most of my colleagues teach at least one of the plays or sonnets and most of them require that their students write essays about their reading, so I honestly thought that reading the work we ourselves generate in our classes would be compelling and instructive for us all.

Unfortunately, this suggestion ended up revealing the emotional temperature of a beleaguered faculty, where any suggestion can spark resentment by sounding like extra work, though I truly intended no extra work.

Right after my colleagues shot down the essay contest suggestion, we received those benchmark tests, along with an additional test to give to our students: a diagnostic test for the California Exit Exam (CAHSEE).

We were instructed to stop what we were doing and take at least six hours (roughly a full week) out of our class time to accommodate these tests. In addition, we were instructed to carve out even more class time to give preparation exercises for upcoming standards tests. And let's not forget that later in the term we would also have to deal with altered and diminished schedules in order to accommodate the roughly three weeks of the actual CAHSEE testing.

Now we will have to use at least two department meetings to assess the benchmark and diagnostic essays. But before we read any of the essays, we will first have to determine appropriate grading criteria.

Assessing our students' writing is the exact task I had suggested in my Shakespeare contest email, but in this case the faculty dread has been fulfilled: extra and irrelevant work, the sanctioned obstruction of any real progress we hoped to make in our classes.

The problem with the CAHSEE diagnostic essay we were asked to give to the students is that in addition to presuming that students know something about global warming, green thinking, and energy conservation, the essay prompt itself was so overwritten that its intention was unclear. We got two different sets of responses from the students: The "Here's why we should conserve energy" essays and the "Here's how to conserve energy" essays, one persuasive, the other expository. So how are we to assess these essays fairly? Do we just look for good, clear, thorough writing? How do we hold students accountable for trying to carefully address a prompt that was not carefully written?

When states and districts lower standards to punch up scores, the tyranny of these scores, which are spun as a district's progress, ends up hindering progress. More important, the tests simply ignore the real grist of any English class-- in-depth reading comprehension, literary analysis, critical thinking, correct mechanics.

Unfortunately all this testing is usually effective in one area: eroding everyone's good will, the teachers' and the students'.

LAND OF NOD (4/11)

Today was one of those days. I thought it would be a quiet day, two classes writing an essay, one class reviewing an essay and thinking about how to rewrite it. But the moon must be full, the stars aligned, hormones in sync. . .

The first class bell rings, I distribute the essay prompts, the kids start writing, and then I hear it. Heavy sighing, loud, dramatic suffering. I finally call the student aside. Tears, fear, more tears. Bell rings, one down.

Then the next class bell rings, and the student in the deepest hole is absent again (absent is that word we use only in school, never in life). Okay, now I have to write a lengthy e-mail to her concerned parent, but twenty minutes later, there she is, standing at my door, still wiping sleep out of her eyes.

The period ends and another girl makes her way to my desk to apologize for her essay. Then waterworks. I find myself saying that she should volunteer somewhere in order to lift her spirits, to help her rise above her feelings. I tell her to put her body where she wants to be and her mind will follow. She repeats the words like a mantra and says she already has ideas about where to start. Crisis averted, maybe.

Meltdown central today and a lots of time

spent counseling and trying not to cry myself.

I should have known the day was off, when I got to work and found that the Dictionary.com word of the day was Land of Nod, the mythical land of sleep.

As a public school teacher, I have spent years taking education classes and attending Professional Development in-services where I have fought sleep while some presenter tries to teach us how to set up vocabulary relay races or how to create "gallery spaces" with huge, wall-size Post-its filled with presumably invaluable student scribbles. I have filled in the boxes for all the "strategies" like "scaffolding" and "backwards planning" and "vertical teaming" on my buzz word bingo card.

Though I have been a teacher for decades, I have never had occasion to use vocabulary relay races or gallery walks, even though the in-service swag—colorful Post-its, pens, markers, glue-sticks--have come in handy.

I tend to leave these sessions in a tizzy. Am I not doing my job well if I do not employ these strategies? I second-guess myself and then struggle to get back on track in my own classes. It's all I can do to remember that unlike these in-service presenters, I don't normally face a docile audience with a high BS tolerance. Instead I teach a complicated, multifaceted subject to a complicated multifaceted group of teens who need to be prodded to learn.

Today's meeting is a refresher on how to teach "Informational Texts," and today's presenters "share" a list of "strategies" designed to teach students how to read "informational texts." If you can get past the phrase "informational text," you are doing better than I am (As I ask every time, aren't all texts informational?). The premise of the session is this: students will not know how to read the deadening texts that the California standardized tests demand the students read, so give them the same kind of deadening texts in class and show the students how to read them.

The strategies are even worse than the premise: Let's break down the reading into sentences and paragraphs; let's make the kids talk in groups about translating and rephrasing these sentences and paragraphs; let's make them learn vocabulary that is unrelated to anything but these sentences and paragraphs. It all sounded like ways to make reading more of a chore than it already is for students already reluctant to read.

Don't get me wrong. I do see the value of teaching kids how to read any text closely. It's just that I am wary about the line between making reading accessible--even enjoyable--and reducing it to nothing more than a chore. I grapple with this distinction in my own classes all the time.

The District has been known to hire teachers

who cannot do the job for which they have been hired, and then spends lots of money and time figuring out ways to make silk purses out of sow's ears. The problem is that those who are teaching well are swept up into that effort at great cost to their time and their morale.

During meetings like this I think too much about the time spent, information gained ratio. I then get to thinking about all the time I sacrifice when I work at home in the evenings and on weekends. It's easy to wonder why anyone would do more than show up in a district where contracts are disregarded, where pay is diminished at will, where no one really has a voice, but most important, where all teachers are treated as if incompetent, and all students treated as if they are stupid.

And then I think to myself, no wonder so many people want to teach--what a great gig for someone who sees it only as a day job with summers off and other lengthy breaks during the year. Why these in-services probably don't even faze them as much as they give them a chance to appear busy.

Just as we teachers are asked to "differentiate instruction," to teach our students based not only on our curriculum, but also on their different learning levels and needs, those in charge never differentiate. So, in a moment of frivolous protest, I ask the presenter, what if I already do a lot of close-reading work in my classes with non-fiction "informational" texts relevant to the literature I teach, like critical essays, reviews, even grammatical instructions? Do I still have to attend this meeting?

 No response.

 Yup, it was meltdown central today, lots of crying and time spent counseling. . . . trying not to cry myself.

NY LOVES ME, ME, ME, ME. . . . . . (5/6)

Today I was walking through the normal crush of students on the quad right before school, and I heard one voice above the rest say to her friend, "Yeah, me and him are goin' after school." Unfortunately, all English teachers respond to such phrasing reflexively, and I have been known to be half-listening in meetings or social gatherings only to suddenly wake up at the sound of a grammar gaffe, and, before I can stop myself, I yell out a correction.

Today, when I heard the grating "Me and him. . .," I did not place a hand on the student's shoulder and gently offer the corrective, "He and I." Instead, I had what I think was an epiphany about why this particular grammatical problem is so pervasive in our culture.

The problem lies in the difference between subject and object. Here is what I tell my students (and remember, by high-school, it's really last-chance grammar, hence the informality):

" 'I' is always a subject; 'I' always DOES the verb, even if the verb is just a state of being: I am, I run, I eat chocolate, I love you! 'I' asserts a self and acts!

'Me,' on the other hand. . . me is NEVER a subject (except when it means only the word 'me.')

'Me' is ALWAYS an object. 'Me' never does anything. Can you ever say (and I say this in my best Bronx meets cavewoman accent),'Me go to movies; me like you; me happy?'"

The kids laugh and laugh, and I think I have made the point. Yet, even without walking through the quad at break time, even in my own classroom after what I think has been my brilliant grammar lesson (as if), I still hear the "me" as subject gaffe peppering the teen-age conversations around me. So what's up?

The Me-Generation may be behind us but the detritus of all those love-thyself-above-all-others movements still haunts us, and, I posit, they have irreparably changed our way of talking about ourselves and our relationship to the world around us.

These days it's all about what's good FOR ME! But look closely at this construction: "Me" is the object of the preposition "for." In fact, "me" is often the object of prepositions: He looks LIKE me; the story is ABOUT me; I want you to go WITH me. Object city!

The "me" gaffe reveals how teens, well, many in our culture, tend to see themselves: we are at the center of all the action, but as passive objects, not as subjects who assert agency by doing or being.

"I" rarely starts the simple declarative sentence anymore and is instead usually used incorrectly at the end of a sentence, as if to strengthen the notion of one's deserving: "That gift is for her and I" or "That is a portrait of him and I" or "Let's keep this a secret between you and I!" Here, the passive "me" just is not strong enough. One needs an "I," a more active recipient.

It turns out the Me-Generation has borne empowered people as much as it has rendered them passive objects. My pal in New York capped this notion for me just today. She writes: "Remember the old "I love (heart symbol) NY" t-shirts? Well, the latest t-shirt sported around town says, "NY loves (heart symbol) ME."

Methinks that sayeth it all.

GRATING GRADING (5/7)

I'm now in my typical weekend perch: a comfortable chair with my lap desk, a stack of papers and an array of colorful fountain pens. I read a story of obsessive love and murder, then another story of obsessive love and murder, then a story about zombies, and another story about zombies.

Amid the many predictable plots that tell me more about the repressed feelings of the students than the actual feelings of their characters, I get to read a story about a girl doing something unthinkable in a school library, two Russians who go to a circus but cannot connect with each other because of the brutality that defines everyone in the story. I read about a dad's suffering over his daughter's choices and about aimless teens reaching out but not connecting. I read about a dissolving marriage and a parthenogenetically born child, a boy in awe of his religious grandfather, a trip to the beach that forever changes two friends, and two children's stories with neat and tidy morals at the end. I read stories about a straight boy singing and a gay boy dreaming. The stories are for the most part well-written, earnest, often moving. Extraneous description, flat characterization, and general aimlessness no longer fill the pages, so I can see the kids have learned something from their workshops.

Though I like to complain to them about having to spend my weekends reading their work, this work is actually lovely to read. Yet somehow I still can't push through all of it; I cannot keep my eyes open. It's May, and I know I am tired, but there may be more to this grading wall.

I have yet to grade stacks of reader responses, where the students were asked respond to the comments I had written on a previous essay and to use their understanding of those comments to redo one of the messier sections of an original essay. I also have to grade reader responses, where the students were asked to select what they think is key text from a reading, analyze it (by identifying and explaining the workings of the figurative language), and discuss the text's relevance to the entire reading. Then for variety's sake, I have to grade first paragraphs and working theses for upcoming essays. In theory, I should be eager to read all this work, to see what these kids have learned this year. But my eyelids start to feel heavy.

    Just as I begin to scan a paper, a beam of sun cracks through the blinds. But I cannot keep my eyes open. Finger yoga, ear squeezing, toe crunching fail, so I get up to sprinkle water on my face, look in the fridge for something to chew, and quickly settle back into the chair. I pick up another page and start to read. The prose soars across the page, the commas are in place, and I feel an A coming on. I read the next few papers with the same fluency, and I can proudly say I am on a roll. Check marks everywhere, high marks all around. Then I get to pages where the student loses himself in the struggle between immense ideas and insufficient writing skills, and my eyes get heavy, my forehead throbs, I cannot keep my eyes open.

    I push myself through a couple more pages and write the usual "Why?" or "Vague!" or "How is the text working?" or "Can you rephrase this?" or "Clarify," "Refine," "Distill," and soon I am not sure whether I am talking about a paper or butter or booze. Truth be told, I am not as bored with their writing as I am with the comments I write. I am tired of seeing the mistakes I have already gone over and over; and I am too tired to correct those mistakes yet again, though I know I will. I am lost in that murky feeling of failure. Then, all at once, whad'ya know, I cannot keep my eyes open.

RIGOR... MORTIS? (5/21)

It's prom night. Most of my seniors are absent, except my first-period Shakespeare students who had to turn in an annotated bibliography for the research paper due next week. I am expecting papers that compare Iago to Milton's Satan; Iago to the Imaginary i (a math student's impressive, if daunting, take); Othello to the nameless protagonist of Ralph Ellison's *Invisible Man*; and the play *Othello* to the *Otello* libretto. I am expecting papers on Othello and the medieval *Dance of Death*; Othello and "blackness"; race as depicted and explored in *Othello,* Amiri Baraka's *Dutchman* and Ralph Ellison's *Invisible Man*. I am expecting papers that compare and contrast the significance of women's roles in tragedy and comedy, as evinced in *Othello, Hamlet, and 12th Night*; papers that trace the development of the staging of Shakespeare's plays; and papers that explore the roots and purposes of the music in Shakespeare's plays.

I am actually looking forward to reading these Shakespeare papers because they will reveal what these students have accomplished after several years of having had the same teacher. This may not be good pedagogy according to some, but for me, it makes for a good test case. My Shakespeare students have worked on research skills, proper manuscript format, how to formulate analytical theses, how to select and analyze textual support, how to convey and respond to arguments for the last three years. Now they get to have the scholar's fun. They get to learn through research, develop their voices, deepen their thinking, and hone their writing skills. Not only can they watch as the professional writers in the academic journals and other critical sources argue about nuances, but they are actually ready to participate in these arguments with their own points of view. I think this is the best any teacher can hope for.

My other elective, Creative Writing, a class that is often a class for slackers who usually don't want to do anything but write the equivalent of "I'm alone, I'm alone, my cat, my cat," has also become a serious academic class, where students whom I have taught for three years generate myriad polished small pieces, two fully work-shopped short stories (one 1500, one 3000 words), several poems in different poetic forms, and two author studies, where they read 800 pages by an author of their choice or an entire collection of poetry by the poet of their choice--all in order to write *New Yorker* style reviews for each. All the work is designed to illuminate, support, and inspire the process of writing.

So why, after building both the Shakespeare

class and the Creative Writing class to reputable numbers--26 in the former, 36 in the latter, do I have to struggle every year to keep the classes alive? Last year, we had an administrator who tried to close the Shakespeare class because the enrollment number of 26 was not high enough to meet the class "norms" (a bizarre word for class-size) that have increased dramatically from the maximum 34 to anywhere from 36-43.

After I told my current students that the classes that they say they love might not be offered next year because I don't have the required 40 students enrolled in each, they told me that they tagged everyone on Facebook and told them to sign up for what they described as important classes. They said several former students, now in college and some graduating, chimed in to say that these classes shaped them as thinkers, writers and as students in general. That is nice to hear and really does validate me enough to enable me to continue grading so much, despite feeling tired all the time. But I still have to ask the painful question: Is the rigor should be sustaining these classes ultimately what's killing them?

Maybe these are better questions:

Does the kind of education that will lead to a diverse and complex life matter? Is it important that education afford one the ability to see the poetry in everything? If so, shouldn't all students be given "access" to this kind of education, this kind of vision starting in 9th grade? And if they are given this "access" early on, would they still shy away from the rigors of a college prep. Creative Writing course or a rigorous Shakespeare course?

    Maybe I have just answered all my other questions.

"AND YOU ALL KNOW, SECURITY IS MORTALS' CHIEFEST ENEMY" (6/12)

When I look at the pictures of suffering sea birds after an oil spill, I see an apt metaphor. I sometimes feel as if I am one of those sea birds, covered in so much muck it's impossible to fly, and that feeling pretty much sums up the reason for my impending departure from the district at the end of this term.

Naturally, I look around at the kids who were counting on me next year, and at the circle of chairs in my room, and I sob. I think about what I will leave behind--a solid reputation, a pretty good schedule, a strong purpose in life that allows me to sleep at night--and I sob. I think about the ease of slipping back into my routine bumps and all next year instead of trying something new, and I sob. I think about the colleagues who understand me and see me as a valuable peer and good friend, and I sob. I think about losing the key to the gate near my classroom, which I finally got after years of begging, and I sob. I think about cleaning out my room and closing the door for the last time, and I sob. . . .

Then I think about what I might be missing next year:

- a culture that uses "data" as if that data were sacrosanct, objective, and instructive,

when it is most often skewed and misleading
- a culture where enormous class size kills the ability to offer class variety
- a culture that doesn't understand that enormous classes will mean that either the lowest or the highest performing kids will be left behind
- a culture where standardized testing eats into so much class time we're really testing the testing, instead of teaching and learning
- a culture that is willfully blind to its tendency to defend and promote only the status quo
- a culture where isolation rather than collegiality is routine
- a culture where administrator and teacher standards vary so widely
- a culture that cannot even begin to address student and parent accountability
- a culture that believes self-esteem is generated by empty praise instead of hard work and genuine accomplishment
- a culture that can neither praise nor punish
- a culture that, to borrow from the late coach John Wooden, mistakes activity for achievement

. . . And I sob.

RECYCLING, 101 (6/19)

    I should be grading my last set of finals, but after emptying file cabinets and book shelves all day, I am coated in sweat and the equivalent of what my dad used to call "purse dust" (you know, the hair strands, lint, tissue, paper, receipt and wrapper scraps that cling to the mints that fall to the bottom of a purse). I suppose it's apt for me to reflect on leaving behind my public school career, at least for a year.
    As usual, my classroom has not been swept in a week, the floor has not been mopped in months, and the only way my desk is cleaned is if I

personally take my napkins and my Formula 409 to it. If I ever see the large, square man they call the Plant Manager, he is usually strolling across the quad at a man of leisure's pace, bluetooth in his ear, phone clipped to his belt. I never see him with a broom or dustpan, screwdriver, hammer, or any other tool of his supposed trade for that matter. Frankly, I almost never see him. So even though there may be a cause other than budget cuts for all the filth that has piled up in my room, after a full day of wading through the detritus of a career well spent, and after sneezing all day from the dust agitation, I am just pooped. Worst of all, I am not even close to finished packing up and getting out of here.

 Fortunately, a few of my extraordinary kids have stuck around this afternoon to help me reduce what had originally been eight boxes of files to three by tossing all but two hard copies of every handout I have amassed over the years. Since I teach in a music magnet, we listened to musical numbers and did our share of dancing around the room-- "It's Too Darned Hot" was a fitting fave-- but we still finished the task, and by the time we finished, we were shin deep in paper.

 One of my kids, a conscientious planet lover who puts me to shame because of her pure-hearted devotion to the cause, piled her car trunk with the ton of paper we tossed. She's going to take it to a recycling center near her home since the school (let's just say if it could make money out of the wasted paper, we'd all be millionaires) keeps its recycling bins locked up and generally inaccessible.

    I can now rest comfortably knowing that paper bags will soon be made of essay prompts on Thoreau and Shakespeare and Poe and Homer; paper cups will soon be made of critical essays about Whitman, Anderson, Hawthorne, Hemingway, Spenser, Petrach, Shelley, Keats; and more will be made out of quizzes and finals and review sheets and short stories and poetry and plays. One can only hope that all the benchmark tests and district directives and other bilge from on high will be turned into its most useful form: toilet paper. I must say, there's something heartening about this recycling notion.
    My kids will also be part of this great recycling in that they will take what I have tried to impart and turn it into part of their ever-evolving perspectives. All week they have been openly

reflecting as they try to hang on to the life and literature lessons they felt were invaluable. They are turning their grief about the end of things into something useful.

The kids have given me photo tributes, flowers, cookies, lemons from which to make lemonade, Reese's cups (they know my pedestrian tastes), unabashed love and tears, even a mock parking ticket on my car, citing me for "excessive grammar corrections." They have come into the room to hang out and to sift through the remnants of my classroom decor. They took whatever was meaningful to them--postcards, statuettes, posters, paper trays, books-- and I was happy to give it all to them. They think my absence will leave a hole in their hearts and should only know the hole they will leave in mine.

It's not to say that my next job won't be good, but I am leaving my current school at the top of my game, so to speak. That I have now been asked to work in a school where I might be treated with a modicum of dignity, along with better hours and stellar colleagues, is no small thing. Right now, however, I am feeling valued all the way around and that is a good way both to leave one job and to start another.

As my students were cleaning out files, in walks a teacher with whom I have a passing relationship. She says, with great surprise in her voice, "I hear you're leaving" to which I nod and look appropriately sad as I wait for some sort of commiseration. I mean, why else would she have walked all the way out to my classroom? Right?

Without missing a beat, she says, "Can I have your file cabinets?"

Then about an hour later, another teacher, whom I have seen only once or twice on the campus, comes out to ask me whether what he had heard about my leaving was true. I told him it was.

"Can I have your file cabinets?"

Let the recycling begin!

REFLECTIONS. . . . .

REWARDS POINTS (1/10)

    One year the mercifully long winter vacation gave me the chance not only to grade 200 pages, to read several of the novels I thought I might have to save until summer, to catch up on hours of sleep, but also to see one of the two movies I usually see per year. And given my ridiculous work schedule, I am usually relegated to choosing a film based more on convenience than anything else.

    Generally, I must say, I am repelled by American movies. For a while there it seemed as if every American film contained the requisite "aren't we all suckers for beautiful young people in love" scene. In these heartwarming films, a restaurant full of all kinds of people, all in unison, and all clearly impelled by the same overwhemling emotion, giddily erupt into some song like "Stop in the Name of Love," and everyone then claps and sings, happy just to be breathing the same air as the beautiful young lovers. UGH! I say.

    When a friend recently asked me what movies I *do* like, I had to say foreign movies, which are usually atmospheric and subtle and don't feel the need to clobber the audience with sing-alongs or sentimental strings or overblown moral or emotional messages (Ennio Morricone and some

Italian cinema excepted).

    Give me a movie like Patrice Leconte's 2002 film "Man on a Train," where Johnny Halladay and Jean Rochefort meet by chance and enter each other's very different lives. Halladay's character is a thief; Rochefort's, a poet and teacher. The scene that exemplifies the kind of subtlety I am talking about occurs when the two have lunch in a local cafe and a young man comes up to Rochefort's character to say that he remembers the teacher and can still recite one of the poems he had been taught. When Rochefort's character, obviously flustered, embarrassed, and proud, asks the young man what he currently does for a living, the man says he works down the street in a lamp shop. No big, dramatic, "You changed my life, and I am now the most successful entrepreneur in the country." No eavesdroppers joining in, clapping and singing, "What the World Needs Now Is Love Sweet Love" or some equally banal gesture. Here the quotidian was colored and warmed for a moment by nostalgia, both the teacher's and the student's, and the connection felt true and, therefore, profound.

    Well, as with all things, one must never say, "Never!" or make sweeping comments based on overblown opinions because one never knows when such broad statements and gestures might come back to, as they say, bite you in the rear, especially when life seems to imitate "art."

During the winter break, I was in Santa Barbara to visit my family. We exchanged gifts for birthdays and other assorted recent holidays and then trundled off to our favorite clothing store to redeem our gift cards. As we moved through the racks, one of the sales women, who offered to set up a changing room for me, could not help grinning at me, her head tilted, a question on her face. After teaching for as long as I have, everyone looks familiar, so I sometimes ignore the impulse to ask people whether I know them, particularly when I'm about 100 miles away from all my teaching experience.

But clearly this young woman and I knew each other, and just as she was about to ask, "Are you...," I asked her whether she had attended the high school where I began my tenure in the District. She was ecstatic when she determined that I was in fact her former English teacher and offered her graduation year and her name.

She then said that my class was life-changing for her, and because of me she had learned two other languages, traveled and studied abroad, and was not just working in this clothing shop, but she was also in school, earning her PhD. She said she would always remember that I told my students never to settle for mediocrity, and that she herself has always lived by this credo. I could not help but hug her at this point, and we both welled up with heartfelt tears.

It was at that moment that I noticed the clicking of hangers and the whooshing of garments had stopped, and all the well-appointed Santa Barbara shoppers stood as if frozen, listening to our conversation.

As my former student wiped away her tears, so, too, did the women in the store, and one whispered to my mother that she had never seen such gratitude or heard such a, dare I say it, heartwarming story before. The whole store had stopped to listen to the story of this grateful student and her humbled teacher. I am happy to report that within moments we were all rifling through the racks again, and no one erupted into song.

I COULD HAVE DANCED ALL NIGHT (1/13)

Often teachers who uphold high standards face students who have no standards. In too many instances students receive inflated grades because standards of excellence vary from year to year, class to class. Add to this disparity the fact that we are smack in the middle of the age of entitlement and its bedfellow, zero accountability, and the classroom can become a treacherous place. When I face students who don't understand why all their "hard work" doesn't instantly add up to A's, I first despair; then I offer this:

I spent several of my formative years in a ballet class designed to groom professional dancers, but even at the tender age of nine, I could tell that with all the hard work in the world, I was not going to be one of those professionals. Yes, I had the grace, the musical sensibilities, but I did not have an instep that started under my knee and an extension that tipped the clouds. Our teacher, Mme. T., was a beautiful, if severe, Russian woman whose days of dance glory had long since passed, but her keen eye and exacting standards dominated the room. She would start us at the barre and would glare at us with her stern, icy blue eyes as she marched around the class in ballet slippers with small wooden heels that clicked ominously with her every step. I remember the terror I would feel as she approached. We were to pull up, to stretch, to point fiercely, to turn out as far as we could. She would sometimes bend down to adjust a curled foot, and she always carried a polished wooden stick that she would use to tap us in whichever areas needed to be reminded to tuck in, straighten up, point hard, and turn out.

After the barre exercises, grueling for their stillness, we would line up to jeté, pirouette, chaîné, pas de bourré across the floor. The class pianist would rev-up, and we each would glide across the floor with as much fleet-footed grace and speed as we could muster. Then would come selection time for the center-of-the-floor exercises. Mme. T. would use her stick to point to us and indicate the spots where we were each to stand for this portion of the class. Invariably, I would make the back row, left corner.

Now, you might ask, did my mother call to complain about the humiliation I must have suffered at being placed in the back of the room for every class? Or did I cry and feel dispirited because I was not making the kind of progress that would put me into the same league as the pre-professionals? Or did I ever say to myself, "This is just too hard, so I am not even going to try!"? Or when I finally realized that I should not continue the classes because they would require too much after-school time for a student not on the professional track, did I say, "Well, since I can't do it, I hate dance! NEVER AGAIN!"? And most important, did I EVER blame Mme T. for upholding standards that I clearly could not meet no matter how hard I tried?

The answer? A resounding NO!

Being in a room with excellence, where nearly unreachable standards were the norm, was a gift. I always knew where I stood, yup, in the back of the room. And I always knew that even if I could not achieve greatness, greatness existed. For me, that was the truest comfort. To this day, I have taught all my classes with this thought in mind: genuine, hard work not empty praise and pandering (whether to students or parents) yields success and self-esteem.

These days the only alumni contributions I make are to that ballet school's scholarship fund; the only cultural contributions I make are to support dance performances in my city; and, of course, I still take dance class three times a week.

WHAT'S LOVE GOT TO DO WITH IT? (3/9)

Recently a former student nominated me for a distinguished teaching award offered by a prestigious American university. This is the second award for which a former student has nominated me in as many years, and for both awards, I have placed in the top 10. For last year's award, I did not make the final cut. My former students said they learned more than they had learned in other classes (an exaggeration all good teachers hear, I know), but they were not members of a disenfranchised urban population, so I did not seem to be performing the kind of miracles one can perform with such a population. Nonetheless, the committee did award us runners-up a decent sum of money for the first time in their history because they felt we were all such strong teachers. That was a true boon.

For the university award, I had a chance to interview with a large panel of influential people. Since some on this panel were graduating seniors, I realized I had a chance to speak my mind to future policy makers. I decided that voicing the issues was more important than being politic and aiming for the win.

As I have said, just the nomination was an immense honor and placing as a finalist is still very moving to me, but what had to be said had to be said. One of the questions posed was a question that lies at the heart of why teachers are often mistreated and always underpaid.

The last interviewer, a wide-eyed university student, asked me this question: "We all know you are a good teacher, but what do you do for your school community?" Yes, she meant besides teach.

As anyone in this profession knows, the implications of such a question are dangerous. First, let's not forget what this profession really entails: prepping, which means closely reading literature and criticism and attending classes and conferences; teaching, which means harnessing the attention of students who often lack impulse control and have no idea what it really means to learn until you have unlocked the gates of understanding for them; grading, which means closely reading and writing detailed responses on reams and reams of paper. Also, let's not forget attending faculty, committee, and professional development meetings, and moonlighting to make up the pay shortfall. This student's question implies that these essential duties of teaching are somehow not enough, that teachers who want to be seen as serious professionals need to be doing more than "just" their "jobs."

Ironically, the implication of the question is that only by extending oneself beyond the profession can one be considered a true professional. Yet, would someone ask a doctor or lawyer what they do for no pay, as if volunteering time outside their professional duties should be a significant part of their professional responsibilities.

This notion of "professional volunteerism" is lethal because it is the reason teachers earn salaries that are in no way commensurate with other "professional" salaries. Stipends for extra work, if offered, are rarely worth the effort. I have never received a stipend for advising the interdisciplinary journal (which I have advised for over 15 years at four different schools and for which we have won prestigious awards each year). Nor did I receive one for the newspaper that I advised. And the tiny stipend I received as a department chair at my former school did not even remotely cover the amount of time and effort I put into the work. It's just expected that teachers will want to do more than what we are actually paid to do, so that's what we do.

We all know that teachers do all the extra work because we are "passionate" about what we do, but more important, we know what needs to be done beyond what our schools and districts are willing to support.

Unfortunately, the interviewer's question plays into the wide-spread cultural expectation that teachers be martyrs for the cause instead of respectable and well-paid professionals doing what all the lip-service says is "the most important and noble work there is!"

The question here is why teachers face this unspoken expectation. I remember several years ago when I taught the incorrigible son of a famous actor, I phoned him with my concern about his son's lack of progress in my class. The actor responded in a very husky and profound voice, "He needs to fall in love with you. If he falls in love with you, only then will he learn from you."

The truth of this answer never left me: Of course, on one level, the actor is unwittingly underscoring the line between pederasty and pedagogy (hence why so many of my colleagues have, over the years, ended up in "rubber rooms" or "on ice" or "paid vacation" until the level of the inappropriate behavior was somehow officially determined). But what he meant is more in keeping with the idea that teachers are idealized parents.

Sudents say, "I LOVE, LOVE, LOVE Ms. _____!" or "Mr. _____ ROCKS. He's the BEST!" or "The only class I get out of bed for is Ms._____'s!" Beloved teachers, like ideal parents, awaken their students' better selves. Or as the actor implied, anyone we love can awaken our better selves.

So it's all about the love, and that's why it's

NOT all about the money. That's why it's all about the unspoken (and sometimes unabashedly spoken) expectation that we serious teachers want to give of ourselves all the time because of all those unquantifiable rewards we receive. . . like all this love.

That's the rock and the hard place where we passionate teachers find ourselves. Shouldn't we merit more pay for this ability to inspire, for this ability to create environments that promote intellectual growth? Isn't teaching, well, enough? Why does motivating students so deeply that they are happy to pour out to us their artless love invalidate our need to be paid well.

You know, I really, really love my doctor… Maybe I should mention this when I ask whether I could just pop in for a check-up?

PLAYS WELL WITH OTHERS (6/26)

What does it take for a person to be someone who "plays well with others"? Does one have to be a leader? A follower? A diplomat? Someone who cares too much? Someone who cares too little? Someone who takes the extra steps? Does one have to be an efficiency expert who sits back and lets everyone else do the work? Someone who volunteers? Or someone who just cooperates?

I myself have been at both ends of the "plays well with others" spectrum, sometimes simultaneously. I've been both selected and eschewed for my leadership skills, selected and eschewed for my vision, selected and eschewed for my punctiliousness, selected and eschewed for just about everything you need in order to play well with others. In my last teaching incarnation I was often considered someone who does not play well with others. Now, several years later, I have actually been on teams that have wanted me as a player, so I think it's time to explore the game a little more closely.

My inability to play well with others with any great consistency could stem from the fact that I've always preferred activities where I compete only with myself-- dancing, swimming, horseback riding, weight-training--to team sports. When I did engage in sports, I was always the last one chosen, after the other side chose the one with the broken arm and the crutches.

  Obviously, the worst player can only benefit by playing well with others. But what about the best players? They can sometimes defeat the team effort when their ambition and skills blind them to the needs of the team. Can the parts ever be greater than the whole in team sports? Does playing well with others mean that one not shine TOO much? Or does it mean that one should shine only if s/he adds his or her luster to everyone's efforts, even the dimmest stars'? Sharing is caring. . . but I'll save that for another discussion.

  I used to get the "you don't play well" jab at conferences or meetings. My heart would sink when, during meetings that always entailed group activities, I was asked to "Share [my] thoughts about [fill in some obvious aspect of student learning] and write those thoughts down on those ginormous POST-ITs to display for a 'Gallery Walk'?" The facilitators would always try to shame everyone into "buy in" by insisting the resistant be "team players," as if being a team player were the litmus test for how well someone functioned as a classroom teacher, locked in a room with 20-40 non-team players. Administrators would insist, "We need to 'play well with others' if we want to be successful!" We do?

While I'm not a team fan, it doesn't mean that I haven't tried to build a team. When I was department chair in my former institution, I did away with paper memos and sent email to my colleagues about anything that pertained to our department. I was aiming for transparency but was greeted with "I get more email from you than people I like" or "I never get your emails because you probably don't have my proper email address, and it's YOUR job to figure out what that email address is!"

I gave up an AP class because other teachers, some with poor reputations amongst both faculty and students but with golden district seniority, were pressuring the administration to rotate the class (not sure where the students' best interest was here, but that's for another essay). Once I let that AP class go, I quickly saw that even with the great success my students had enjoyed each year, I was probably not going to get the class back. Then, I realized that by giving up the AP class, I had set myself up for even greater insult: the electives I had created, Creative Writing and Shakespeare, were also on the chopping block--classes I had worked hard to prepare and build to substantial numbers each year, but weak by my school's enrollment standards.

I had taken not only one, but two and three for the team, and I had to ask myself, for which team?

By offering electives to the students who wanted a wider range of rigorous English courses designed to prepare them well for college, I would not be available to teach the general English classes. Since the number of students who wanted the electives was smaller than the number who needed to be placed somewhere, anywhere, the students who wanted to take my courses were sacrificed for the sake of the team--but again which team? The team of administrators trying to find the most gutless and efficient way to place what they saw only as student bodies into classrooms with interchangeable teachers? The team of teachers vying for the best students under the guise of "doing what's best for the students"? Or the team of students attending school in order to get a good education?

Not only did I wonder which team I was on, more important, I had to wonder why all these factions weren't part of the same team. By asking such questions, I was immediately accused of being one who "does not play well with others" or is not a "team player." Then again, what kind of team would cut down its players like that? I know. . . teams that aren't really teams in the first place.

According to HR websites, playing well with others means bringing solutions to meetings, communicating effectively and positively with coworkers, sharing success and credit for that success, keeping commitments, generating trust by not blaming or blindsiding coworkers. But none of this can happen if we don't answer the one essential question: How can anyone play well with others who don't share the same vision and values? The answer to that question became increasingly obvious to me, so I packed up my toys and took them to a different sandbox.

I have learned I can be a team player. . . but only when a team is really a team.

YUP, IT'S JUNE! (6/28)

I can safely say I made the right decision to leave public school. After leaving, for the first couple of years, I sat on the sidelines as I watched my former colleagues receive seniority-based RIF (Reduction in Force) notices, better known as "pink slips," furlough days, and other veiled threats to their well-being in the wake of deep public-school budget cuts. As usual, much of what was threatened was restored by some last minute "windfall": pink slips were rescinded, the number of furlough days reduced, health care untouched (even though the providers themselves continue to diminish the benefit of "benefits"). All this sturm and drang has taught teachers that there must be large and powerful conspiracies at work, so they should simply keep their heads down and toil in isolation in a system that doesn't really count them as much.

The sad fact is the yearly budget cuts are the only part of the system that puts teachers first--they are the first to face untenable class sizes, reduced supplies, and RIF notices. Teachers no longer unite to gain ground; instead, in isolation they lose ground. Workable class sizes, a genuine voice in school policies, sabbaticals, a guaranteed, comfortable retirement are quaint notions of the past. The "Windfall Elimination Provision" makes it impossible for teachers to collect both their teacher's retirement and the Social Security benefits they may have earned as viable members of the workforce outside public school teaching. Yes, CEOs can get their billion dollar bonuses, but those teachers better not double dip, even if they are dipping into funds they have earned!

So as teachers fight for their dignity, the District can force its ideas about testing down their throats without rebellion or even complaint; it can continue to hold teachers accountable for forces beyond any teachers' control (a students' family life, for example); and it can continue to expect teachers to take the abuse of students, parents, and administrators without any real protection.

"If it's not broken, break it" rules the day, and teachers can either avert their eyes as the crushing wheels continue to turn or leave. That's why I left. After the second of two 10-year stints in the District, I "graduated" with the kids I first met when they entered my 9th grade class four years earlier.

The first year at the new school had its challenges to be sure. Every new teacher must be tested, even if she is a respected veteran teacher, new only to the school. And tested I was. Students who were asked to work harder than they had ever worked before and parents whose shame or guilt overrode their good judgment tried hard to denigrate me and diminish the standards I had set, standards that have always helped students. But I fought back by being as determined, consistent, and fair as possible. Naturally, once the students saw that they had actually learned something, their fear evaporated, their hearts and minds opened, and the year ended much better than it started.

EPILOGUE:

Unlike my experience in public school, where students crammed into my classes because they wanted to learn as much as possible, in my current school, initially students had crammed into my classes for precisely the opposite reason—they thought they could manhandle me into letting them coast. They soon learned that that I was much firmer than they had expected. Many students I had my first year went on to challenge themselves in my AP classes, and those who could not meet the standards as effectively started to understand there were standards to be met.

It has been eight years since I left the District, and I would be lying if I said it has been easy. But I get to work with a strong faculty and an administration who share and support my goals and the standards I uphold. So for now, I am part of a good team.

No teaching job is without its challenges, but as I have learned from riding horses these last several years, keep your head up, look in the direction you are headed, and always remember, FORWARD IS YOUR FRIEND!

This book is dedicated to my students, just as I am.

Made in the USA
San Bernardino, CA
17 November 2018